Made in the USA
Middletown, DE
05 October 2021

You are the star of this fucking show.

Take revenge and shut the fuck up.

The ahorita tiempo is now!

Unfortunately, God kills heroes and fools alike.

You might have plans
but the ultimate plan belongs to God.
- Jesus

Your only weapon really is patience.

Pride won't help you get what you want.

Freedom is the destiny of the soul.

This water I hear, this fire I feel, this air I breathe,
this earth under my feet, have been here forever.
They are eternal and I am part of that eternity.

I wish we didn't have to stay up all night to get lucky.

Back then we had each other,
now we have lots of things.

My art wasn't going anywhere
until I started painting cats.

It's a great canvas, very large, a masterpiece.
If you get tired of it, later on,
you can have your kids paint on it.

Be nice — it's easier on you.

The guy with the gun is always right,
unless, of course, you have a rifle.

After all this pushing and shoving
we all end up as plant fertilizer.

Damn, I feel so disgruntled,
and I'm not even an employee.

Keep your heart more like a river and less like a lagoon.

Not even in my dreams can I get what I want.

Every age comes with its own fears.

Don't be angry, it gives you wrinkles.

Old folks are always shaking their heads in disapproval
as if we were in constant need to please them.

You want to converse with someone with a brain in LA...
pick up a book.

The great teaching of the East is to dismantle the ego while the one of the West is to build it up.

There's a lot more random than the predestined ideology
the conspiracy theorists are so in love with.

America's such a go-getter culture
even happiness has to be a pursuit.

America has very successfully transformed
every single citizen into a consumer.

Damn, it has been a roller-coaster and not of love!

Darling, there's nothing wrong with you,
you're just on the wrong medications.

I got no layers; I'm a millennial.

For some reason millennials respond very well
to the word deconstruct.

The feeling you get when you walk down the self-help section in a bookstore and every title applies to you.

The only reason I can deal with LA
is that half of it is water.

'Mericans are heroes and superheroes
only in the movies.

What really fucked up this world is this idea
of constant achievement.

…and that annoying tech/startup crowd
with their "game changer, disrupting the industry
unicorn" bullshit.

These fucking millennials; they're covered in tattoos
yet they haven't been anywhere, definitely not jail.

What the fuck are you honking for?
Don't you see I'm editing my playlist!

The most dangerous vehicles in California are:
any off duty Metro® bus, beige Volvo® station wagons
(usually full of boxes and cats), Saturns®
and Mongols® on Sundays.

These Trader Joe's® employees are so nice...
they make me feel like I'm evil.

Omg, I'm starting to look like
those before pictures in gym ads.

It's important to have something to look forward to...
like death.

I'm demoralized, depressed, discouraged...
basically everything that's starts with d.

I grew up analog, yo.

Amazing, like the smell of cotton candy.

We're all searching for God,
I wonder what's God searching for?

Why are the French so enamored
with Existentialism?
Americans, on the other hand,
fell in love with unhinged, unprecedented,
unraveling and disrupting.

I want a free refill!

Americans are so naive;
they think it's burned toast that will give them cancer.

To have a successful book it has to be about a girl;
usually a girl on something or with something.
So I'm working on two new books:
"Girl on a Cactus" and
"The Girl with the Pink Rabbit."

I've been waiting for my comeback
for a long time now.

Why does the vision of future
have to be always dystopian?

I hope you were drunk when you got that tattoo.

Why are American politicians so in love
with "make no mistake"?

Homelessness and crime are simply
the byproduct capitalism.

Suddenly every idiot in America is an activist.

People forget that Columbus
never wanted to come to 'Merica.
He wanted to go to India
and find enlightenment.

...but I like nonsense; our dreams are made of it.

Well, even dogs are delusional;
look at a poodle bark at a pit bull.

I'm finally feeling optimistic
because worse than this...
something good is bound to happen.

Don't tell me you're gender neutral.

I bitch, therefore I am.

It's not that I'm unfriendly,
it's that these people are so uninteresting.

There's so much of our parents in us
that to be mad at them is senseless.

Happiness is that sweet spot
between anger and depression.

People tell me you I shouldn't drink by myself
but what about all the friends that show up
after the first bottle.

Buddhism is about finding the right balance between
doing nothing and not doing anything.

Americans went from 'united we sit' to 'united we fuck shit up'. I don't know if that's an improvement.

California is so empty everyone is looking for meaning
but you don't have to be a clairvoyant
to see through the bullshit.

She's cute 'n' all;
I just hope she doesn't go all 'Amber Heard' on you.

I used to love women before moving to LA.

This galaxy sucks.

The light from the sun takes 8.5 minutes
to reach the earth. The sun doesn't know it.

.

God will remind you who the boss is.

The problem is not death,
it's that we think we'll live forever.

I have a serious plan for each one of you,
now where did I put it?  - God

Don't be too optimistic.

Change comes from within, and from within
a nice house in Malibu is a lot easier.

White liberals matter.

I only realized she was talking about a dog after she said, "and finally he stopped peeing in the house."

I'm all-spiritual but that new Celine® bag...

Bitch, don't you know I'm a Jedi. - Episode X

Are you like,
a gender-neutral, sex positive, feminist,
latinx, non-binary pansexual?

Ahh...the feeling you get
when all of your devices are powered up.

The problem with technology
is that we're making each other obsolete.

Americans, seem to be all stuck in high school;
the few that make it out remain in college
for the rest of their lives.

In America, you drive inland twenty minutes
and it goes redneck very quickly.

Fuck all that up and down — I'm on Lithium®.

I need to get back to my angry self,
this depression is killing me.

Are you, like, a sex-positive feminist, gender neutral, latinx, non-binary pansexual?

Live for the Likes!

Women spend half their lives ignoring men and the other half complaining about them.

Everything you'll ever need is inside of you.

I don't understand people that say,
"I don't drink because I get a headache the day after."
It's like saying, "I don't work out because
I feel sore the next day."

Art is fine but liquor is quicker.

Getting things right is not easy.
God's been at it for millions of years.

Forget about finding the one,
I'm happy with the second or the third.

The world, beyond the myth of success, wealth
and fame, has been lengthily steeped in insecurity,
egotistic narcissism and fear. In a daily battle,
(armed with delusion, gossip and pseudo spirituality)
we fight the horror of self-insignificance.

.

Living with fear is like riding a bicycle
and worrying that you could get a flat at any time.

Women are all feminists until the bill comes.

If the glass is half empty,
open another bottle and fill it up.

We're all equal on the dance floor,
except for the ones who dance better.

I love technology;
when I talk to myself people think I'm on the phone.

What doesn't kill you makes you stranger.

Damn, you're so enlightened
I have to wear sunglasses around you.

The world will always have an appetite for the new.

I just have the pre-existing condition
of being pissed off.

I did that DNA test and it came out
that I'm related to coffee beans.

There's got to be a support animal out there for you.

I'm glad this summer is over,
now I can be properly depressed
and not feel weird about it.

Once you realize you'll be unhappy anywhere,
then you'll be happy everywhere.

The worst part of globalization is that even European porn stars started to say 'oh my god'.

Americans are so bored they will sue themselves
to make things happen.

If you keep seeing a palm tree,
you must be doing something right.

Don't tinder and drive!

She was really fit and sharp
when she was on that methamphetamine diet.

He seemed very charismatic and intelligent
until he started talking about aliens.

The sauce on the meatballs is always red.

The only important thing about the past
is that it brought you here.

It's never too late to become a cat lady.

It's nice to know your friends
are nowhere to be found
when you need them.

I hear a few inner voices
and they're all saying fuck you.

Damn, my reservoir of hate is almost full.

When you tell a joke to a German,
he doesn't laugh, he says: "That's funny."

Talking to a German is like talking to Siri
only with a Schwarzenegger's accent.

If a tree falls in a forest
and ruins your marijuana plants,
does it make a sound? No but you will.

She went to India to find enlightenment,
but she got hit by a bus instead.

Don't worry about being vegan;
you might come back as a soccer ball.

You didn't have to eat that burrito.

Where would we be without fashion? Omg...
we'd be still wearing pants and dresses.

Getting older is like taking a disco nap
and waking up the day after.

I succeeded.

I failed.

So what...even God comes quickly!

Death is issue-free.

Be the change.
Omg, I change, like, three times a day.

When they say we only use 10% of our brain...
it's especially true in LA.

Omg, that's some white trash saga!

I mean bad...like old men with ponytails.

Happiness is just like puzzle that's impossible
to complete because you are missing a few pieces.

...ooh, just the usual seesaw of anxiety and regret.

I drank so much coffee today,
my bathroom smell like Starbucks.

Omg, LA has made me a misogynist.

"It smells like nail polish," "It's graffiti bitch."

I saw a beautiful old tree and I thought,
wow, no one stops to admire a young one.

Fuck that hubris, we're all in the hands of God.

Not the entire universe is on your schedule.

Usually when women say, "I know what I want,"
they mean they want it all.

In LA, they all have a chip on their shoulder
for being neither rich nor famous.

I hope you have all your essential oils, bitch.

The most important thing in life
is having a laugh with your friends.

…and quietly repeat after me. "What the fuck did I do?"

Regrets are annoying and twisted little paths that fork into a myriad of other even narrower meaningless paths that lead nowhere.

That goody-goody stuff makes me car sick.
There's still nothing like murder and mayhem.

I know we discussed this
but when we did, I was really drunk.

I'm no longer interested in any situation that's no longer beneficial to me. That doesn't necessarily mean I've become a selfish asshole.

You were special.

The Buddha Represents !

You can either look at two hawks playing in the sky
or at the scratches on your bumper.

Always trust your instincts,
and see what God throws your way.

Don't just sit there and feel bad about yourself;
go out and make someone else
feel bad about themselves.

You're as honest with me as you are with the IRS.

·

I had so many good ideas,
and I'm glad someone else is doing them.

The subconscious is terribly overrated.
Not to mention the silly stuff
it constantly comes up with.

Being depressed is ok,
just keep it one notch over suicidal.

…don't eat those gummy bears while you're driving.

The politically correct quotes
of the artist sometimes known
as Michele Castagnetti

abridged

Anno Domini MMXXI

The truth or something else will set you free.

I hate people — they're everywhere.

I really need to get off the grid
but I'm worried there won't be any wifi out there.

I'm not selfish — I'm self-involved.

What the fuck am I doing here?
I should be over there.

A squirrel crosses the street and gets run over, it's random. A person crosses the street and gets run over, it's destiny.

It's hard to be stimulated by the Californian flip-flop crowd unless you're talking movies, sports or aliens.

Do aliens have a bible?

I know the poison; I just don't have the antidote.